REST FOR THE WICKED

Glyn Maxwell

ERIC BLOO DAXE

BLOODAXE BOOKS

ISBN: 1 85224 295 8

First published 1995 by
Bloodaxe Books Ltd,
P.O. Box 1SN,
Newcastle upon Tyne NE99 1SN.

Bloodaxe Books Ltd acknowledges
the financial assistance of Northern Arts.

Cover printing by J. Thomson Colour Printers Ltd, Glasgow.

Printed in Great Britain by
Cromwell Press Ltd, Broughton Gifford, Melksham, Wiltshire.

Acknowledgements

Acknowledgements are due to the editors of the following publications in which some of these poems first appeared: *Forward Book of Poetry 1994* (Forward Publishing, 1992), *The Guardian*, *The Independent*, *The Independent on Sunday*, *Jewels and Binoculars* (Stride/ Westwords, 1993), *London Review of Books*, *Manhattan Review* (USA), *The New Poetry* (Bloodaxe Books, 1993), *New Statesman & Society*, *The New Yorker*, *The Observer*, *Poetry Review*, *Poetry with an Edge* (Bloodaxe Books, new edition, 1993), *The Rialto*, *Sibila* (Madrid), *The Spectator*, *The Sunday Times*, *The Times Literary Supplement*, *Trafika* (Prague) and *Verse*.

The poem series 'Phaeton and the Chariot of the Sun' was written for *After Ovid: New Metamorphoses* (Faber, 1994). 'The Stakes' was commissioned for *The Bookworm* (BBC Television) and first published in the race guide at Newmarket. 'Yellow Plates' was written for *Klaonica: Poems for Bosnia* (Bloodaxe Books/ *The Independent*, 1993).

Contents

Peter Brook

Let every page
Begin as clean
And end as clear
As stories are
If actors pass
Through pain and grace
To make a stage
Of any place.

Let every word
Be prized enough
Shyly to talk
Or weep with work
Or fail afresh
Towards a truth
That may be heard
Beyond its breath.

Let every gap
And every strip
Of space fulfil
Its hapless will
That all about
Each uttered mark
The matter drop
Into the dark.

Let every line
In ignorance
Of whence it came
Or what's to come
Hold out its hands
Into the breeze
As I do mine
And cling to these.

The Ginger-Haired in Heaven

Sometimes only the ginger-haired in Heaven
can help me with my life. The flock of blondes
is sailing by so painlessly forgiven,
still blinking with love no one understands,

while the brunettes float thinking by the rushes
long after what they chose, long reconciled,
and here, the fair and sandy, all their wishes
half-granted them, half-wish them on a child.

Only the ginger-haired remember this, though:
this sulk and temper in the school of Time,
this speckled hope and shyness at a window
as sunlight beats and blames and beckons. I'm

not coming out. They won't come out of Heaven,
or not until with auburn in the blood
two mortal tempers melt together. Even
then we might stay here if you said we could.

Rest for the Wicked

We only know we've come to the end of something
by our meeting happily here. Because when we were young,
even the end of a termtime, a school play, a holiday,
would splash us away towards love, hearts wrapped, some hero.
And our goodbyes made us sniff because they weren't true,
those tears of incompatible salt-group A –
we *do* know the group we are, we are all O
why else is the world still turning, I ask? I do know –
when we parted we went with the force of fifty greetings.
Today we greet with the strain of some mere losses,
with compound eyes in which all the darkly envisioned
watch with us, and a loop and whorl of a language
which always gives us away or shows what we came to,
or shows we know it was only the end we came to.

The Passing Picture

When lovers twist apart on benches
    Through remainders of Septembers
All the tense who stride beyond them
    Group their thoughts in sudden children's
Crocodiles and lead them quickly
    Home into some silent reading.

When lovers stretch in two at stations
    All the passing picture journeys
Lasting longer hours than England
    Has, wide afternoons of strangers
Sunned and staring back, decisive.
    All determine this shall happen.

When up the aisle that all expected
    Lovers inch and cities time them
Now for once, for now, is seen
    Who walks a line that leads uniquely
On, and who, like thought, meanders,
    Fading like a loss to science.

When in remainders of Septembers
    Lovers twist on benches, sprawl,
Or stagger home on England, don't
    Believe the mathematics ever
Frees the music. All that wander
    That way wander straight as starlight.

The Wish

Alone in spoiling it, I said I wish
That I can wish for everything. They said
That's cheating. You've one wish. I said that *is*
One wish. We sat against the paper shed.

They, who had wished for peace on earth, for painted
Chocolate cities, flights to anywhere,
And one strange one to play with *her* (they pointed
To where she did her handstands on her hair,

Her pout flipped to a smile, as if the sky
Would grant what it amused itself to grant)
They pondered, troubled, hot with how and why,
Considering my case. When the bell went

Against my wish and that most amazing field
Began to be abandoned, as that girl
Was falling to her feet, and chocolate filled
The hands and crumbled happily, I was still

Wondering, as I was all afternoon,
If they would grant my wish. When at last they would,
I found myself at my own gate, alone,
Unwishing, backwards, everything I could.

Self-Portrait with Softball

Settling down on that royal field I refuse
To believe you have not imagined in your town
(It's not there now and never was, never mind
You saw it, sat there, dug your spade in the sand
And blinked in a well of sunlight) I noticed a man
Pacing along with a purpose a little surprising
On this hot turnabout day of a central year
In western civilisation. Must have a plan,
You noted and I snorted, while, all around him,
The hoops and balls, frisbees and boomerangs
Catapulted and curled but he kept his line,
Dressed as we'd all be dressed in a week or so, tending
His itches as he had to, tugging his collar
To feel the air when it got around to breathing,
Making his way out of sight. We were keen to know him
Before he got that far, and the way we did so
Was when from the hub of the hottest of many thousand
Games on the green a ball bounced into his arms
And he stopped, that focused us with a foreign stillness.
Slowly like anyone else that afternoon
He was happy to hand it back, though not before
Appearing to be confused that everywhere
The games went on so widespread and regardless,
Milling and marvelling out to a bluer haze
And on. Nothing had stopped as dead as he had.
Nobody young ran up and depended on him.
Only the sun and us had observed the help
He was still so keen to offer, glancing around,
Hoping to find some match that couldn't restart
Without this thing in his hands. But there wasn't one.
The games had changed because of him but went on
Without him. It was his seeming not to have got this,
His standing reading names on the ball like a headcase,
That made us grin and remember what his job was,
And clunk our cups of picnic fizz and forget him.

Birth Day

Through light so nursery-bright on a playing field,
Soup-tin red, sea blue when the sea was really,
Greens of the good for you or a game played fair,
She walked with a smile between the deliberate rings
Of the cross good children shyly ignoring her.

Her young black hair was tied back in a headscarf;
She looked ahead at the houses, though her eyes
Were dark and distant with remembered hymns
Begun inside. She was believed by it all,
Now weekdays whirled and the news of a boy or a girl
Joked in her brilliant blood.
                              And the glamorous cars
In glossy maroons and greens and stripes went by,
And smokers born in a blanket in a grey war

Bought rainbow-shimmering records and sportsman cards,
Bright paperbacks with jazzily slanting words,
Chewed and swore with a grin then stared all around
At the light all cherry colour.
                              The whole world over
Nations hastily, scrappily, sulkily born
Pretended they'd been sitting there, honest, forever,
And every oblivious woman and innocent man
Glanced up from the work in hand on the world's one town –
Verges, roses, pinning up, setting out, hosing down,
Whatever. Time began.

As You Walk Out One Morning

Brrring. It is the day of your Proposal.
Get up. You're on your own. You are a suitor.
Leave your attic, basement, croft or castle
In AD, BC, either. Doesn't matter.

A to B is indeed the way you are going,
Towards Before, appropriately enough,
As they do say how it wallops your sense of timing,
Twangs that nought-degree meridian. Love.

You note at once that no one is beside you.
Your neighbour said he'd wave, but so far hasn't.
'Our blessings! May our God be there to guide you!'
Your family never said, and their God isn't.

Your street curled up like it shouldn't have been in the sun.
The houses waddled away, and your underclothes
Are hitching home together. You've got on
A suit you never liked and suppose she loathes.

The bus conductor is me. My bus remains
Beside a depot and both are yet to be thought of.
The road likewise is a field and awaits the Romans.
You wear on your wrist a sundial and it's sort of

Stopped. The craft you became superbly skilled in
Over the years is of no use to any.
Your parents have decided against children.
Plantagenets are peering from your money.

The Earth is of course quite flat, and the heavenly bodies
Twinkle explicably. One is as big as a Swatch.
Today they are all gone away, gone away where God is,
Where the dead play whist and the unborn ask can they watch.

Everyman is still on a final shortlist
In that young kingdom, Fellowship and Good Deeds,
Friendship, Knowledge and all of the Devil's hitlist
Are still his friend, and he himself still God's.

But you, it is the day of your Proposal.
You feel the Dead Sea lap the palm of your hand.
Your heart is as light, your soul as white as Persil,
The world and weather more like this ordinary brand.

Flatness on which you travel, height that picks you
Out as a Possible, width that introduces
Infinite manners of *no*, and a breath that sucks you
Up to a point: you have all these, and voices.

Voices! Low in the raincloud flutter the wings
Of *what* and *where* and *why*, the loquacious dove
She-said-to-me, that craps.these green new findings
You pause to analyse on your own sleeve.

These you have. But, when you search for the face
You swear you pictured, all the others who ever
Put in a brief appearance in that space
Rustle like actresses to the scene, and pucker.

So all that's left of the love that yesterday
Filled the world is a porch with a bell and a wait,
The number-whatever of here – though who's to say
What squiggles mean? – and the yellow or green or white

Or black or some other word of the closed door.
This, when it opens, frames you into a suitor
Earnestly of your century, the Before
Prattling on at the steps of your mouth, and the Future

Playing it clever and cool in your brown eyes.
The Only Girl In The World arrives to assess
Whether the Future infers what the Past implies.
With all respect, don't hold your breath for a yes.

Love Made Yeah

First and zillionth my eyes meet eyes
        unturnable from, unstarable in.
Whoever was marched from the Square of my reason
and to what court, I don't give a hyphen
        va t'en to the King!

Our drapeaux are waving and what's in the offing
        but tears, tribunals and unwelcome aid?
Nothing but glorious, jealous, incredulous,
bibulous, fabulous, devil'll envy us
        love made, love made!

'Yeah,' but you say, with the Press of the planet,
        'Look how it turns out: the heroes felled
in the upshot, the oiliest climb of the customary
bourgeois fuckers as easy as muttering
        argent, ackers, geld...'

Uh-huh, sans doute. But here at the heart
        of the movement I trust my hand in another!
So CNN tells me I'm odds-on to cop it?
That ain't news, guys, I did arrive here
        via a mother.

No, when the Square is dead again, but
        for some oligarchy or puppet or shah,
and I'm banged up and on trial in slippers
for following, wishing on, crediting, catching
        her my star –

don't do the pity. All right, do the pity,
        but that won't happen, believe it from me!
Her eyes are as hot as one needs to ignite
the cave in the human guy. I am hers,
        friends, I am history!

Among Equals

Now here he comes who came from almost nothing.
He has to be the captain of no comment.
No fault of his his car is made of something
Pluto's made of, nor that this shit morning
Is spitting tears at him like a grappled student,
As here he comes, grey-suited, sealed, unsmiling.
What cracks a smile is when he sees us coming,
Our lenses glancing up from nothing doing
To crowd him, have him smile until it hurts him,
Until his teeth are cold and we're still laughing,
Still working, powered up and in position.
It's when he's out of range or out of picture
We can it, and the tools of our profession,
Still throbbing with the clubs that wouldn't have them,
Or writhing to the click of a clear future,
Flop out on passenger seats, get some shut-eye.

Either

A northern hill aghast with weather
Scolds and lets me hurry over.
Someone phoned to tell my father
Someone died this morning of a
Stroke. The news has tapped me with a
Stick. I vaguely knew his brother.
No one knows where I am either.

Now I'm lost. I don't know whether
This road runs along the river
Far enough. I miss my lover,
Town and all the south. I'd rather
Die than be away forever,
What's the difference. Here's another
Field I don't remember either.

Platform Piece

Love, which is the hand at the carriage window
taken, stroked, touched, held and then held on to
until it has to

wave with every stranger waving also,
writes letters in a café now. It lingers
always in this misremembered city
of still canals reflecting the green lamplight,
will trace initials in a filthy ashtray,
or take some colder hand in its cold fingers
to stroll along those lapping watersides
perhaps a mile at midnight.

Then part all of a sudden and be waving,
enthusiastic, positive with pity,
so waving with all strangers waving also,
so many waving now it comes to nothing,
and nothing keeps you riffling through these postcards
till rails tear you blinking from that city.

Conquest

His house, his town, his garden, his own room
Sprout with memory, jungle-green and seething.
He was a Spaniard, gilded and immune.
Now he's a native, sickly and just breathing.

Five Old Games

The game is that you don't step on a crack.
    And when you do you're dead, so when you do,
You lie. You say whoever says you did,
    He is a liar. Then when you get him back
And he complains, you say he's a liar, he would,
    Until they weary and agree with you.

The game is that you're first to over there.
    And, if you can't be, stop when you're halfway,
And watch the others lose the joy of it
    And struggle with their weight in the greased air.
Thus, as their wasted breath is leaking out
    All yours is saved, as you're about to say.

The game is that you keep to the white square.
    And, if you don't, you lose, so when you slip
You sob in an enormous cracking voice
    You didn't understand, it's never fair,
And look, you're bleeding now. You pull the face
    They don't forget. You foam at them. You flip.

The game is that you stay away from it.
    It's got the plague, it's got the germ, and when
It gets you and you get it, you say no,
    You say it's wrong, it's not a thing you get.
You had your fingers crossed against it. So.
    It sniffs and shrugs. It won't try you again.

The game is that you run away and hide,
    But have to, if you're found – you will be found –
Look everywhere for everyone, so when
    That happens close your eyes, stay there, be dead,
Until they show up, angry with you. Then
    Just watch them come and pull you from the ground.

State of the Nation

Now any word from you is a new word,
As gnarled and unawaited as the new
Could ever be, the tongue of the grim few
Who burnt my flag, and I did have a flag.
I had, like we all have, the shape of shroud
Or swaddling with me gone from it. That flag.

And any news of you is propaganda.
In that I can believe it well enough,
Or that it was concocted by your staff
To be believed. All but the oldest pictures
We mock as forgeries, and my children wonder
What I am always burning and I go *Witches*.

No, I have let them clean across my country,
The people of your land, in happier times.
I've neither known nor cared about their crimes,
But neither have I let them stay. I trust
They know the points of exit and of entry
Can still be told apart in the red dust.

And yes, I have corresponded with your greats,
Translated work, remembered stanzas, lines,
Partaken of your wisdom as your wines,
And told my countrymen: They are the Past,
But they had jokes and hopes and secret dates,
They thought their paste-and-paper homes would last,

And that their prayers were heard. – But it's the Law,
Or is it here. Your earth is blown and lost.
You work forever in a birdless west
In binary. You will not be received.
Your immigrants will be turned out at door,
Their fantasies and nothing else believed.

Your treasures we will lick into clean plates,
And wring the loaded clouds so very tight
They bulge apart and wash your picnics out,
We sorely hope. Our likeliest to die
Will dream you up when he hallucinates.
The best of us will cross and pass you by.

But don't assume we do this to our other
Neighbour, where they whistle the To-Come.
Her citizens are made to feel at home
As long as they require it. They belong.
All borders are the same, except the border
Between our kind and you. That's barbed and strung,

Uncrossable, too long for the pinched age
We have as nations. Say there's still some meadow
Where we could meet or send in place a shadow
To make the signs we would. That would be news.
Perhaps in your gone country there's a stage
For puppetry. It would at least amuse.

My motorcade went miles along the border
One April night. I listened and saw nothing.
Then there was distant rocketfire, then nothing,
A pitiless cold dark. It's said we're winning
(Admittedly by me, and it's an order)
But when the morning breaks I think we're winning,

The salmon light falls freshly on the schools
I built, and loyal students in the squares
Are gulping down espressos as I pass,
And every evening all the theatres shine
With characters we know and love, and tales
That never were, but happen, and are mine.

Away But Always

Your beasts are in the garden with their maker,
And that's how it should be. There are no friends,
No jokers and no lovers on this acre.
It ends because it ends because it ends.

Breathe or don't, it floats away without you,
It twists and catches, floats up into space,
Away, but always stubbornly about you,
Beyond you as the young and faded face
The absent know you by.
                    The closest creature
Knows you better, knows you by the sound
Of grinding on the hot lathe of the future,
And sight of sparks you cry to the cold ground.

Stargazing

The night is fine and dry. It falls and spreads
the cold sky with a million opposites
that, for a moment, seem like a million souls
and soon, none, and then, for what seems a long time,
one. Then of course it spins. What is better to do
than string out over the infinite dead spaces
the ancient beasts and spearmen of the human
mind, and, if not the real ones, new ones?

But, try making them clear to one you love –
whoever is standing by you is one you love
when pinioned by the stars – you will find it quite
impossible, but like her more for thinking
she sees that constellation.

After the wave of pain, you will turn to her
and, in an instant, change the universe
to a sky you were glad you came outside to see.

This is the act of all the descended gods
of every age and creed: to weary of all
that never ends, to take a human hand,
and go back into the house.

Epithalamium: The Boys and Girls of There

(for Stephen and Sarah Mead)

The grasses were as ever the first to know,
    but gossiping they just leant and listened and nodded,
        absorbed it into their posture, and forgot it.

The cedars remembered hearing it once before
    but they hadn't believed it then and did not now,
        when the robin said 'Do you think so?' 'We know so.'

So the robin as brown as earth had nothing to tell
    the few of that desert town, though his chest was taut
        with wanting to, and the oldest woman he met

observed this, stopped, and guessed her improbable guess.
    Silence grew some twenty-four bare arms
        sweeping the road of the town with whispering brooms

till a paler path was cut through a sea of dust.
    Last from the cool dry huts were the vigorous men,
        still proud but with all hope and pity gone,

wiping their palms in anger and terror at this
    sweeping work, then the whole town stared up the lane
        at something striding out of the hammered sun

the shape of a single person bound in a wheel
    that rolled away, and he stayed three days in the place.
        All they remembered afterwards was his voice,

no help to the Romans, less to the man they sent
    from Herod equipped with a looking-glass from China,
        who herded them up and said 'Look I have forever

so take your time.' But what was there to remember?
    Though they might hang for forgetting the words he spoke,
        his name at the very least, the point of his work,

their minds were blank, they were bright but blank, they were bright,
and all they would say was 'Yes, he was here, he came,'
and what was his name? 'Ask that bird for his name!'

but the robin as brown as earth flew bursting away
with something to tell elsewhere, while the cedars sighed
'Yes, we were wrong, but we abide, we abide,'

and the elders dozed, but a boy and a girl of there
sprang to each other and stared, for their being apart
was a wound they would have to mend, and they made a start.

The Stakes

Forget that in the three-fifteen
My love was quartered pink and green,
Had cherry sleeves and epaulettes

And blinkers and a poet's name.
Forget it couldn't fail but came
Nowhere. In the five to four

Forget my love was gold and grey
And thundered recklessly away
But tired and didn't place. Forget

The diamonds and diabolos
And checks and chevrons of all those
Who caught my eye, engaged my hand

And lost my stake. It's ten past five.
My love is emerald-starred, and me I've
Set my house and bet my heart

On what reminds me of my love.
I know that's going to mean enough.
The gods of form and fortune know

I will not lose. Now off they go.

Song of the Sash

So when for the once in a life I again find you,
    And my heart says *Go!* to my mind not the other way round,
And my mind had already gone without being told to,
    And my heart is free, or free with a single bound,

And the ones of the past are hobbies of rainy summers,
    And the ones of the future hurry away like spies,
And the interested draw near and go smirking from us,
    For life is us and the rest well-intentioned lies,

What I shall do is rush from my home right here,
    And lose no time in packing or food or the fare,
But grin in the mirror, vanish and reappear
    Under the clock on King of the Castle Square.

King of the Castle Square will be dark with men –
    It always is, the wives are about their meals –
It's the men who muster to march and who say when
    To start out for the Dirty Rascal Fields.

The Dirty Rascal Fields are the homes of any
    Who run away, you watch, they are never there.
The men believe they are organised and many,
    They leave the world so often and so bare.

As the march begins, I will dash to the very top,
    And whom will I find but the leader of all these men,
And what will I do but demand of him that he stop,
    And what will he say but *It's him, it's a thief again!*

His sash I will take, his sash with the things it means,
    I'll snip it away and be gone where it doesn't mean them,
And find where you live down narrow unchanging lanes
    No man with a sash has marched on, none has seen them,

And you I will wrap in the sash if it goes with you –
    If it doesn't I'll find some other parade to run with –
We'll wait on deserted fields in the first of blue
    For what remains of the men when the marching's done with.

Growing Men

Unravelling red carpets for ourselves,
We're nudged and turn and recognise each other
Stooped and grinning. Slowly we straighten up,
Praise to the sky what sky we see in any,
Then stand on these red carpets for ourselves
All stinking good and spreading out like lives.

The lamps were low enough, the riling heat
Was blood itself it fuelled us so fully.
Whoever did this had to and knew how to.
Whoever did this ought to wipe the ceiling,
Because we're taller even than our heat:
We top it now, our temples lit with sweat,

Our heads of jungle hair congealing, set,
Our thoughts old, crackling thoughts. Pick one, pick all.
Discarding all but one you're stuck with all,
You darling gardeners spotlit on a stroll,
You giant bending angels. You are set
To want us. In that moment you forget

Your eyes are not the eye we inch towards.
Your smell is nothing but a mask of rain.
Your mouth is not our dream of the great well,
And we grow stupidly and proudly from you,
Grow coldly, undramatically towards
The best we get: to nod amid the clouds.

For now we sleep or seethe. We are always young,
And always saddening in our eagerness.
Whoever did this ought to break the glass
We'll grow so high, so high we'll see he has –
He broke a star of air when he was young,
Quite carefully, as if he'd wait that long.

The Night Is Young

I was with some friends when I noticed with some strangers
One of the Gang. And we rose like we'd won awards,
Reluctant and delighted, to a position
Halfway between our tables, and began,
Began with a tale of now and ourselves, but soon
Were hurrying back in the years like children yelled
Out of the light of their inexplicable game,
Into the brooding houses to be held.

Nothing's changed, we said, since everything had.
Again some time, we agreed, as it never would.
When I sipped and caught him searching my eyes for the kind
I was, he caught me searching his for the same.

Though my new friends and his, from time to time,
Would look across and point out a seat in the ring
For either stranger, no, we remained right there,
Steadily finishing off what was there to be said,
Drinking and putting our tankards down slowly.

And when there was nothing listing the names like somehow
They'd be around us. the Gang, like the night there was no one
Missing. Weren't we over there by the window?

I'd seen some, but he'd seen two I expected
Never to see again, they were fine, they were fine,
He mentioned, and that was that.
                              I returned to my circle,
Shaking him off as doubtless he shook me off,
Answering who he was with an oh someone,
Settling to the night, uncomfortable, gruff,
And feeling about as young as the night is young,
And wanting it all, like one who has had enough.
You don't forgive what's left of what you loved.

A Swing from Gotham Central

The man whose fault the rain is is smiling through it.
The woman who parked her wagon first is the woman
Who wants to go now. Ellie, who made the banner,

Is tripping up over it in it; her children who baked
The flan have completed eating it, and the Count
Whose money it was is selling it in the rain.

But the man whose fault that is is smiling through that,
Sharing a loss that the rest of the world elected
Not to share, as the short and tall of the village,

Spiking the litter together, scowl and avoid
Each other's patches. And each other's surnames
Except to answer the question 'Whose fault was that?'

So this is the Evergreen Party the morning after
The crucial votes of the village's great old oak
And those of its leaves and the usually solid ashes,

Beeches, elms and sycamores were counted.
They all recall it was at around four-thirty
The woods declared and showed. 'Showed brown as the heart.

Brown as the broken heart. After all our work.'
'Don't get me wrong, they've a right to vote as they like.
Don't get me wrong.' 'They're firewood.' Young volunteers

Tearfully pick the beige slips from the meadow
And stare at them or fold them and let them fall.
The candidate stands in his green suit under a willow.

Here comes the No More Rain Till Judgement Day
Action Committee, braving the slant of the drizzle,
As in the distance the Flat Earth Front cry 'Hey!'

And signal exaggeratedly Thumbs Downs
To their backers lowering square binoculars.
People are gradually going away. Where to?

Here, where the tree with the bluebird in it is ringed
By a wicket fence hand-painted by a farm boy
To stop the bluebird running away when it wakes.

Museum

Sundays, like a stanza break
 Or shower's end of all applause,
For some old unexplaining sake
 The optimistic tread these shores,
As lonely as the dead awake
 Or God among the dinosaurs.

Old Shepard and the Sale

Here, along a bright blue-carpeted passage
inside this tallest shop in the capital,
up steps the ancient pride and joke of the firm:
old Shepard in his uniform. For the Sale

begins today and he moves to the double doors.
The mob pauses and heaves, and turns its head
to say to itself to behave and it heaves again.
It gets its signal from Big Ben but Shepard,

bigger far in his pride of place, just smiles
his jailer's grin and taps the face of his watch.
Like saying Time is here not there. Inside
there trembles crockery magnified in each

aiming, narrowing eye, and all assistants
brace themselves like sons of William Tell.
Old Shepard starts eliminating keys
from his enquiries, drops them, sees he will

yes pick them up, sort out the one he thinks
opens the doors. He tries it and it works.
He steps aside. The free go gurgling past,
as waters into gutterings and cracks.

The Furthest West

You lot got dazzled and burned
All afternoon. We two were last to arrive,
Tipsy and hand in hand
And, if they go, and they do, will be last to leave.

The rocks encroach and the Cornish sand stretches
Where we settle. This
Is the furthest west she says she has gone for ages,
Which isn't true, I think, but I say yes.

Blues emerge and blur, like the promenade sketcher
Couldn't do edges well and thought
A vague, dark and watery picture
The pricier art.

Fine constellations spoil his plan. I
Sweep them up in my right hand.
More grains in here, you know, than stars in the sky.
Yes, she says with a sniff. Other way round.

Now the sea goes quiet, straining to hear
Our shared and differing views.
Then gathers, rolling, breaking clean out of nowhere
Its only news.

Watching Over

Elated by ourselves, we shift and slip –
Mouths open with the memory of a kiss –
Parting in two to sleep, and if it's mine

Then that was it, that break above, and now
It's yours I wake to witness your unknowing
Our love and all you know.
                                    Some ancient will,
Though night is safe and quiet here, commands
You be watched over now, and, to that end,
Exacerbates the wind and whipping rains,
Or amplifies the howls of animals
To make my waking watchful and tense,
Though for a thousand miles there is no mind
To hurt you, nor one raindrop on the wind.

The Dark Flower

The wizard in daylight stoops to the dark flower
And picks it, killing it, sniffs it. All of an hour
He's circled here, he's puzzled the dry birds
Who circle us, he's lost them for their words.

They'll land and walk, you watch, they'll walk away.
I, like a lucky page, have words to say
In earnest question but they shy in thought,
Because I learned from him what he never taught:

Words are the world without him, with him gone.
But he moves among them, stared or smiled upon
Like any human dwarfed in a deep grove
Of marble figures. Nothing will be enough

For men abandoned to this magic. Night
Discovers them in shapes of a same plight,
Loved and applauded in unpeopled lairs,
Wishing the magic was, or wasn't, theirs.

Invigilation

There was barely a one among them who thought he needed
The three whole hours allowed. After say two,
Big papers started to bloom. I went out to collect them.

Divested of their petals the candidates each
Sank back dead with a sigh and the clock went suddenly
Still unsure who was asking what, so it just

Went if they weren't looking and not if they were.
I, having cruised this test in an earlier life,
Saw rhombuses in my name and coloured them in.

Until as there always is there was only one,
One in the light, on the spot, while the rest of them stared
In exasperation escalating to anger,

Not that after their answers a slower answer
Was worming across a space, but that that answer
Was jogging the world and it was too late to right it.

The Boys at Twilight

Alive to the lilac, dead to the blue,
Bees in the act till the lilac's through,
There's a boy with you and a boy with you.

And the boy with you as the sun goes red
And the lamps go rose and the old to bed
Has remembered words you forgot you said.

If the time comes up when the mind is ruled
Then the nastiest face you have ever pulled
Can't winch you clear of his lost new world,

Can't free him or loose him or let him forget
He's the luckiest boy you have ever met
If the time comes up when the heart is set.

You can pass him lies like so much slack.
You can mouth to his bearers behind his back.
You can fake with a passion and love with a knack

It's hopeless. But hopelessness full of hope
Is the serious man on the end of the rope,
Is the ring and the race and the telescope,

Is the gibbering soul at the outhouse door,
Is the flapping aloft and the crawling ashore,
Is the meaning and matching and marching to war

All hopefulness. In the looks of the shy
Look clear through the fog and be certain why
When the galaxy lunges across that sky

The boys flare up with a hapless glow,
And follow it out to a woods they know
Green-smelling and smothered as years ago.

They sleep in the cold unswayable sight
Of all they envisage, the giant delight
That itself feels nothing but a scratching, slight

But not giving up. Oh, wipe them away.
There a boy tomorrow and a boy today,
Words they are going to remember to say, /

Hopes they are going to remember from when
They have no idea but they feel them again,
Who are going to be boys, who have had to be men.

Song of Our Man

By light of what when filtered down
The piling jungle must have been –
    Once – the moon,
Between what stings and what is silent,
Off the undisputed island
    Swarms the dark platoon.

That was some-worse-where we never
Even thought of, chewing over
    The worst things.
These were who, when cracked reporters
Bared the facts at yellow waters
    Glittered in the wings.

Beyond obituary, they
Inhabited what wasn't Day
    Or Book, or Sun.
Or sound. Or the right words for words,
Or anything our old accords
    Were predicated on.

That was them. We knew their track,
That ultimately they would back
    To a red moat:
For there was only this much left,
The valleys stitched, the woods bereft,
    Our man in the last boat.

But what we didn't know, they were.
What we don't believe, they are.
    There they are.
Out floating out and still alive.
We will breathe and cock and drive
    But not, now, far.

The Sentence

Lied to like a judge I stepped down.
My court cleared to the shrieks of the set free.
I know the truth, I know its level sound.
It didn't speak, or didn't speak to me.

The jury caught the tan of her bright look,
The ushers smoothed her path and bowed aside,
The lawyers watched her fingers as she took
Three solemn vows, her lipstick as she lied.

She vowed and lied to me and won her case.
I'm glad she won. I wouldn't have had her led
However gently into the shrunken space
I'd opened for her. There. There now it's said,

Said in this chamber where I sleep of old,
Alone with books and sprawling robes and scent.
With all I have, I have no power to hold
The innocent or the found innocent.

Lust

Lust is at home here and I make it welcome.
I offer it stuff it accepts but would otherwise take.
    Beautiful telling ache.
Lust will be last to leave this all-nite affair,
    Make no mistake,
    And it was welcome,
    But I live here.

Six for the Wicked

Some came entitled to regret,
    All left as proud as men can get.
Some slunk in dark along a wall,
    All left in shades, forgiven all.

Some came resolved and some reviled,
    All left remodelled and restyled.
Some brought a stash to make amends,
    All left with more and many friends.

Some bowed their heads remembering,
    All left reliving everything.
Some came for keeps, to grow, to grieve.
    All left, or are about to leave.

What Thought Is Not

It won't allow you rest, but, after all,
It's only Thought. It may run up and tug you
Frowning through arcades of fuming trash,
Evaluating all in a curt breath,
Or shut you in a spire like nobody
We've met, or it may drive you over moors
Bad company in the back. Whatever it is,
Thought, it's not what roars up in a group,
Out of a blue you hadn't noticed, sets you
Shrugging where you never were but are now,
Pours into your palms its mainly broken
Trinkets, makes a waltzer of your shadow,
Then waits for the great staggered loud arrival
Of those it telephoned, just on the offchance
That they were in, and free, and liked surprises.

Garden City Quatrains

First day of school. A boy looks through a pane.
This is the end of freedom, not a visit.
The King's Cross-York-Newcastle-Scotland train
Slams through Welwyn Garden and I miss it.

*

1880. This asthmatic geezer
Home from Nebraska batters down a map.
Says Bernard Shaw, 'What's up there, Ebenezer?'
'Quiet,' says Howard, 'I think I've found a gap.'

*

By all means vanish, shrug and with a sniff
Explain your town is dead, that anywhere
You're not a native must be filled with life.
Remember where you're gone is the thin air.

*

Woods were north. The south was all my schools.
East was alien housing, west I knew.
Start of a poet. All the rest is false
Or true extrapolations of the view.

*

An idiot asks to know the route I run.
I say I start at home, head north until
Ayot Green, then turn back for the town
And home. He scoffs: 'So more or less downhill.'

*

ST ALBANS KILLED WELWYN is what is written
Under the A1(M). And WANKY SHIT.
In the United Kingdom of Great Britain
And Northern Ireland that just about covers it.

*

'How's "Welwyn Garden City"?' It's the same.
How are your parents? Sticking with that old
Mum and Dad of yours? Still use a name?
Still born in late September? Hoch, I'm called.

*

Our nearest Lord has turned the nearest park
Over to golf. Between his pits of sand,
Six proud walkers hold their thread of path
And stamp it so they know where they can stand.

*

Through marvellous locked gates, one has a view
Of his grand Hall, along a splendid drive.
I saw in early April '92
A poster. Guess. No. Conservative.

*

A Martian Votes in Welwyn-Hatfield

Inhabitants converge upon a shed
One by one all day, to make a cross.
Outside their homes some show their feelings. Red
For really cross, yellow for fairly cross.

*

The Coronation Fountain in the centre
Of town has been switched off. The Council said
It cost too much to run, what with the winter.
[That's enough royal allegory. Ed.]

*

The Observation of Mr Lohn

Before the night begins, my friend and I
Stop outside the autobank. I run
To take out forty quid. We drive away.
'Out stealing from yourself again, eh Glyn?'

*

They lost their nerve in 1970.
'It's neither Welwyn, a garden, nor a city.'
They thought up 'Howardstown' and 'Waverley'
Since nothing had these names and they were pretty.

*

Western Garden Citizen, I stand
At midnight in the east and say 'I'm lost.'
But I'm starting to get to know the back of my hand,
At the cost of moving on, which is no cost.

*

Small hours. The tots are in their cots. The old
Are in their homes. The thin Nabisco towers
Snore the malt. Two strangers have and hold,
And, as in real places, something flowers.

*

Who's in the kitchen? London, the life and soul
You weary of, flirtatious, loud, and hot.
A young well-meaning man is in the hall.
He's got his gift and bottle. What have you got?

Not You But Something

Warm, a July, and a day that burrows through.
You hurry on. It seems this is a place
You ought to leave behind. You wonder why
The locals stick around in watching groups,
        Watching for what? Not you:
Something expected, bloated, bad, nearby.

So then you swat the breeze and papers, stare
Off somewhere unconvincingly, or tread
The stones uphill. And all the flags are twigs,
The statues loll, the pigeons peck around them
        Looking for what? Not you there:
Something enormous, bald and bare, that digs.

Girls in the smell of this are the second worst
Thing to a family moaned at through a gauze.
Foreign here, but they're foreign everywhere,
Girls. Your hopes go cold as kids, go by
        Remembering what? Not you first,
Something expanding but just sitting there.

The afternoon will lope if you wait so long,
But you won't wait so it won't lope. You turn,
Ignored among exhibits, let through gates,
And meet yourself in a mirror, gelling the hair,
        Ready for anything. Wrong:
Something alone that bitches and imitates.

Burrow, burrow, until and beyond what light
There'll be – you get sucked headlong, do you recall?
Where lamps are hooked, and eyes cry out, intent,
Adoring what you mean, like the lucky stars
        That passed on the cold night
You were what came, was gratified, and went.

If You Haven't Got a Shilling

Christmas came so fast around the corner
We concluded we were lost or perhaps had taken
A misdirection when we'd stopped and spoken
Thankfully to the kindliest-looking stranger.
Perhaps we'd been too thankful to be listening.

Our youngest throat had barely healed from singing,
Our oldest eye from a twinkle. Certain of us
Had said goodbye for good and all to Christmas,
But there nevertheless he was, planting and grinning.
I did hear shouts behind us: 'What's the hold-up?'

As we bumped into each other as we pulled up.
Neighbour and neighbour nudged and were crying 'Humbug!'
Or saying 'I'm Dutch if it is!' then 'Eat your homburg!'
When clearly it was. So kids were heaved and held up
To stare comprehendingly at the hinting visage.

We sat down gladly, chuckling back the message,
Greeted with some hysteria, some corpsing,
Indubitably some embarrassment at his timing,
But largely with goodwill. After all, the passage
Is not his fault, his business, or our business.

'Well, if he says so, fine!' was the consensus.
We'll do our bit, we always have, we want to!
We told him we all wondered where he went to
Every year, which brought a tear to Christmas,
Because he really thinks we do all wonder.

The Plot and None

When all the plays you had ever seen saw you
go reading through their rooms and gardens, no one
overtly commented on it, only the few
you'd played, whose lines you'd learned or were working on,
dried on some orange-highlighted riposte.

The virtuous non-speaking wished you well
the way they do, unceasingly, while the host
went smirking to the wings of his white hell
to hiss and come back charming.
                              But to what?
The lines were striking but the room was still,
light draining through some fissure in the plot,
and none came to the reading of the will,
or really loved, or looked to hear the shot,
but sat there satisfied or, even worse,
went smiling to the lip of the lit stage

and on, oblivious, starting to disperse
among ourselves, unpeeling from each page
as all of us do always, leaving, One:
some barmy and inexplicable carry-on
directed shrilly from true darkness. Two:
you, or this local amateur cast as you.

Songs from Plays

1 *Harvest Song*

Start where you stop,
    Hoist the high hoop
Day, night and crop
    From a skip to a stoop,
Jump through the ring
    Day, night, everything,
Jump through the ring,
    Priest, peasant, king,
Until all pass through
    Then I'll jump through too.

The Hawthorn go by,
    Good fortune in May,
The green Elderflower
    Jump through, jump through!
Dark Elderwood too,
    The Judas Tree,
Leap through the hour
    And be memory.

Go by, by St John,
    Herb-Robert in June
And the Roses ablaze,
    Jump through, jump through!
Wild Strawberry too,
    And on Midsummer Night
Leap high through the haze
    And be gone from sight.

Go by, the dry hay
    Through a yellow July
And the Queen-of-the-Meadow
    Jump through, jump through!
The good Wormwood too,
    At the Dog Day Fair,
Leap and your shadow
    Will lose you there.

Go by, the great Harvest,
    Go by, golden August,
The corn in the light
    Jump through, jump through!
The Silverweed too,
    Black Poppy and beer,
Leap the blue night
    And tomorrow is here.

The fairs of September
    Go by, now the summer
Is home from the day,
    Jump through, jump through!
And the Hazelnut too,
    And the Blackberries in,
Leap clear into May
    And my song will begin.

Start where you stop,
    Hoist the high hoop
Day, night and crop
    From a skip to a stoop,
Jump through the ring,
    Day, night, everything,
Jump through the ring,
    Priest, peasant, king,
Until all pass through,
    Then I'll jump through too.

[FROM *Wolfpit*, Act I, scene i]

II *The Bones of Summer*

Sloes and ciders, pigs and bloodlet,
    Over and ember,
    Over and ember,
In by the door when the frost is moonlit,
    White is the fruit,
    White is the fruit,
White is the fruit on the bones of summer.

58

Plums and damsons, quince and offal,
    Over and ember,
    Over and ember,
Stagger in cold with the last of the windfall,
    Black is the wind,
    Black is the wind,
Black is the wind through the bones of summer.

Flames and stories, witch and whisper,
    Over and ember,
    Over and ember,
Eyes of the dead in the cackling timber,
    Gone is her love,
    Gone is her love,
Gone is her love as the bones of summer.

Friends and frenzies, ale and firelight,
    Over and ember,
    Over and ember,
Dance to my arms in the mist at midnight,
    Bright is our fire,
    Bright is our fire,
Bright is our fire with the bones of summer!

[FROM *Wolfpit*, Act II, scene i]

III *New Year Song*

The apple's eaten, the year is died,
The sun is climbing over the side,
The sparrow's flown the ocean wide,
    Remember me, forget me.

Gather in rings and part in pairs,
And ring the days and part the years,
Twinkle from another's tears,
    Remember me, forget me.

Old Year left my love for dead,
New Year see me wooed and wed,
For all was said that will be said,
    Remember me, forget me.

Cold is life but living burns,
Winter rakes but Spring returns,
Then Summer sweats till Autumn yearns,
    Remember me, forget me.

Fresh is dawn and pale and rose
With blood of Time, but no one knows
Where Time or Love or Laughter goes,
    Remember me, forget me.

The apple's eaten, the year is died,
The sun is climbing over the side,
The sparrow's flown the ocean wide,
    Remember me, forget me.

Tom Parch's Midnight Verses

The year's a hag, the night is young,
The thief is stole, the sheep is hung,
The song is plucked, the carcass sung,
    Remember me, forget me!

The year's a man, the night's a maid,
The thief is cooked, the sheep is paid,
The lady's done, the deed is laid,
    Remember me, forget me!

The year's a babe, the night's a crone,
The thieves in flocks, the sheep alone,
The crop is shat, the crap is sown,
    Remember me, forget me!

[FROM *Wolfpit*, Act III, scene i-ii]

60

IV *Jill-go-by-the-hedge*

She said the violets never flower
    Upon her window ledge,
She said the crocuses would wither
    Round her garden's edge,
She said I was her Valentine,
I said was I? She wasn't mine
    So Ladysmock and Cuckoo Pint
    And Jill-go-by-the-hedge.

Ladysmock grows soft and pink
    Upon her window ledge,
But see the throbbing Cuckoo Pint
    About the forest edge,
She bade me pick the Pint for her,
I said I had one, she said Where?
    So Ladysmock and Cuckoo Pint
    And Jill-go-by-the-hedge.

The evening's long and light again
    Outside the window ledge,
And midges merge and spiders spin
    Around the meadow edge,
I went with her as far as this,
But don't you ask how far that is,
I'll take it out and point and piss
    On Ladysmock and Cuckoo Pint
    And Jill-go-by-the-hedge.

Jills, your Jacks are going by
    Below your window ledge,
And sigh and breathe and breathe and sigh
    About your garden's edge,
And breathe and sigh and blow and suck
And lick their lips and try their luck
So ask them up to pick and pluck
    The Ladysmock and Cuckoo Pint
    And Jill-go-by-the-hedge!

[FROM *Wolfpit*, Act IV, scene i]

v *Song of Inspector Fykke*

The Murder of Cyrus Lockweed? Solved.
Dr McCollar with a poisoned leek.
The Murder of Eustace Witbert? Solved.
Marcia de Gruse with a lump of teak.
The Murder of Maisie Hatchet-Peters?
The gardener Plummer with pinking shears.
The Murder of Clyve, Lord Quick of the Feathers?
His butler Pierre who had loved him for years.

What was his one mistake? The moonlight.
What was her motive? Rank jealousy.
How did he kill her? A lens and the sunlight.
How did you know it? How do you do it?
The answer was clear for you all to see.

The Clubbing of Princess Imelda of Tyre?
Digney the diplomat, easily caught.
The Loss of the Laird of Lamminghamshire?
The Countess of Rogering, fainted in court.
The Aubergine Murders? Quentin Du Pré.
The Parchment Stabbings? The Reverend Clay.
Death in the Larder? Schmidt, with his tins.
Murder at Croquet? The Bagburd Twins.

What was their one mistake? That parrot.
What was his motive? Consuming greed.
How did she kill them? The phial in the carrot.
How did you know it? How do you do it?
The answer was plain for you all to read.

The Slaughter of half of the vicars in Essex?
Most of the others, they fled on a train.
The Hacking to death of the Dean of Wessex?
He did it himself, an insurance claim.
Death in the Cloisters? Brother Martinus.
Death in the Convent? Sister Simone.
Death in the Night Sky? Zardoq of Venus.
Death in Eternity? God On His Own.

What was his one mistake? I was watching.
What was their motive? To catch me out.
How will we kill them? By making and stretching
A rope all the way from the top of my thinking
Down into England and pulling it tight!

[FROM *Whodunit? Who cares!*, Act I, scene iv]

Crackdown

We know what you're out there up to.
You're up to the evil that has to be put a stop to.

We know why you do it, too.
You're bad inside. There's bad, and it got in you.

You won't get what you want.
We're decent and *we* don't always get what we want,

But you'll get the opposite.
You'll get ten, twenty years of not having it.

So will the ones you love.
So will the ones you sob at your photos of.

So will the dump you're from.
Be blue light of the 21st century, chum,

The day you hobble free. Free?
Too good for you, that. Not good enough for me.

Curse on a Child

*Darlin', think of me as a stopping train. I go all
the way, but you can get off anywhere you like.*
MALE ADVANCE, OVERHEARD

May the love of your life get on at Ongar
And wake up sleeping on Terminal 4.
May his anorak grow big with jotters
Noting the numbers of trains he saw.
May he read these out in a reedy voice,
May he drink real ale with his mates while you
Blink in the smoke. May his hair be a joke.
May his happiest hour have been spent in Crewe.

May he call for you in a lime-green van,
May his innermost thoughts be anyone's guess.
May his answer to 'Who's your favourite band?'
Be the only occasion he answers 'YES,'
But then may he add, 'When Wakeman was with 'em,'
And play you the evidence. May what he wears
Never again be in vogue. May his mother
Dote, devote, and move in downstairs.

May your French turn frog, may your croissant go straight,
May your bread be Hovis, your wine home-made,
May your spice be Old Spice, your only lingerie
Les fronts-igrec, and your beauty fade.
May you curl in the Land of Nod like the child
You were when you wouldn't, and screamed all the way
From Perpignan to the Gare de Lyon,
Echoed through Paris, and on to Calais.

The man in the corner, who sat with his head
Awake in his hands, has issued this curse.
He is far away now. What keeps him awake
Isn't screaming, or crying, or writing verse.
It is sometimes nothing but quiet, sloping,
My terrible infant, looming and deep.
May you never know it. May your life be as boring
As men can make it, but, dear, may you sleep.

Don't Waste Your Breath

On sales or sermons at my door,
Contributions from the floor,
    Screaming things.
Wondering where the good times went,
Complaining to this Government,
    Reciting 'Kings'.

Telling fibs to Sherlock Holmes,
Games of tag with garden gnomes,
    Soliloquies.
Knock-knock jokes on a Croatian,
Great ideas for situation
    Comedies.

Asking her to reconsider
Leaving, trying to kid a kidder,
    Roundelays.
Entering for field events,
Just causes or impediments
    On wedding days.

Begging rides in backs of hearses,
Happy Birthday's other verses,
    Asking twice.
Musing on your point-blank misses,
Moaning 'This is hell' or 'This is
    Paradise.'

Offering a monk your ticket,
Using metaphors from cricket
    When in Texas.
Telephoning during finals,
Remonstrating in urinals
    With your Exes.

Phrases like 'Here's what I think',
Giving up girls/smoking/drink
     At New Year.
Asserting that all men are equal,
Settling down to write a sequel
     To *King Lear*.

Revisions to *The Odyssey*,
Improvements on Psalm 23
     Or hazel eyes.
Glueing back the arms on Venus,
Any other rhyme than 'penis',
     The Turner Prize.

Interrogating diplomats,
Defining Liberal Democrats,
     Begging to banks.
Supporting Malta's football team,
Translating King's 'I have a dream'
     Into the Manx.

Reading verse to lesser mammals,
Tailing cats or humping camels,
     Hectoring sheep.
Pleading with a traffic warden,
Writing things that sound like Auden
     In his sleep.

Don't waste your breath on telling me
My purpose, point or pedigree
     Or wit or worth.
Don't waste your breath explaining how
A poem works, or should do now
     You're on the Earth.

Don't waste your breath on rage, regret
Or ridicule; don't force or fret,
     Breathe easily.
Remember: every starlit suck
Is seven trillion parts good luck
     To one part me.

Tycoon

Known by the shortest of three Christian names,
He rolls his sleeves and goes the distance. Laws
Like two commissionaires let him through, his claims
A fraction over half-convincing both,
And money opens the doors that open doors
As sure as gut and throat make way for vomit.

Nothing stands in the way of the whole truth,
His readers know, so when he comes to the rim
Of the whole truth there'll be nothing to speak for him,
Let alone save him from it.

Blue Sky Raining

From what they did they walk exonerated
        one dark evening.
The gathered have to suck at the stopped air.
        That this will not
be tried because too many know or care

shocks only idiots nowadays. They walk
        from what they did
exonerated not in law but fact.
        A puff of chalk dust
wipes reports already halfway written.

They squash escorted on through cameras
        flashing but then
lurching backwards like some panicked troop
        uncaptained and afraid
of the uniform and jaw of the just cleared.

They stroll a blade of silence to their black
        and black-windowed cars.
From in them, each a king as all are kings
        who one dark evening
drive from what they did exonerated,

they see you people, shocked to be found no whiter
        than they are, scratch,
get heaved away like heartburn. One detective,
        innocently settled
to hear all human speech shrink to confession,

as lies have been and fact will be and soon
        silence, disappears
into his vast suburban fortress, just
        as rain begins
to fall like rain that means to fall for years.

The Margit-Isle

(for Patrick Howarth)

The boy had died. We knew that right away.
'Es gibt kein Luft,' I said. On a cold day
We should have seen his breath as a cone of mist.
I was proud I'd used some German words. We stood
In a park in Budapest.

        Some passers-by
Did just that with a glance. The German fat guy
Peered and shrugged and went. A flashy rich
Prostitute arrived. She was the first
And only one to touch.

        It was 2 pm.
Nothing happened. 'The police are going to come,
And we've no papers,' I fretted. Patrick said:
'They won't ask anything,' and an ambulance
Braked and no one did.

        They hauled him up.
His anorak hood fell back. Our little group
Saw now he was a girl. She could have died
Of drugs or cold, stabwound or rope or rape.
Least bad was suicide.

        They drove away.
We'll never know a thing. We spent the day
In the tight conspiracy of private shocks.
A clerk in police HQ would make some notes
And slide them in a box.

        A year and a half
And I'd do this, predictably enough.
In Hungary perhaps they shed some light
On why she died, but light shed on a death
Is not what I call light.

I was waiting.
To bring some writer's thinking to the writing.
Of what it was to chance on the fresh dead
In public in broad daylight in the middle
Of where we are. Instead

It's ended up as dry as a lucky stone.
Something to carry around and feel. Move on.

The Great Detectives

None can leap as far as the great detectives.
Not only can they bare the cause as if
It stripped itself in public, they can sniff
Effects it never had till now, or motives
Stuffed in coats, contemptibly denied
By those who did it, know it, and can't hide.

None can sleep as light as the great sleuths.
To them the stars are evidence, the moon
A gaping witness and the nightmares soon
Resolved into incriminating truths.
The corn of life is twisted into scenes.
Who have the time and reason have the means.

Who hangs about that drawing-room alone?
None now, where failures trot to the great chair
And ring around its ankles like a fair.
Then everything is epilogue, is known.
After the accusation's shot and stuck,
Who's left will make an innocence of luck.

No certainties like those of private eyes,
Once the detecting bug is coughed and caught:
Whatever art is made, or history taught,
What isn't Law might just as well be lies
For all the help it brings in the hot nights
Before the white steam clears and he alights.

No charm like his, no eccentricities
So crisp, authenticating and sincere.
And, as for her, who would have thought it here?
That one could solve so many with such ease?
But better turn those hooks and curious eyes
To joyful exclamations of surprise!

The truth is out with murder and with blood.
They drape across the sofas of the town.
Whatever may be used is taken down.
A friend runs into strangers in a wood.
He shrugs the shoulders that the earth has picked
To flop upon and sleep. In the next act

The corpse is quiet. Once the avenging eyes
Have gone out for each other and for good,
The guiltlessness will swell like a flash flood
And thunder as it must, where the land lies
Low and weak, then crack out to the sea
That mutters Hamlet's question endlessly.

The great detectives of our time we'll never
See at first hand, ours is a later book.
We don't know how it ends though we do look,
Climb nervously ahead to the dust cover
And peer at names. We can't expect the murder.
We must be those who don't. We're not the reader:

We have to cast about this ancient pile
Without a host, and make our plans together;
Or sleep alone and dream of one another,
And pause in all its chambers for a while,
Lift every implement, have every cause,
Be watched in silence through the double doors.

We have to know we could appear to be
Accomplice, alibi or, munching there,
The thirteenth guest who's welcome to his chair,
For how we need him in our company.
But, when the porch is darkened with the shape
Of hat and stick, of case and folded cape,

When all are drawn towards him in a room,
As shadows of suspicion fall like cards,
When some are lost and some are lost for words,
And some, forgetting, gratefully assume –
Be out of that dead chapter like the clues
He couldn't understand, so couldn't use.

The Devil at War

That truce didn't last.
    The dark school dropped its people on to the road
Like dice cast
    Loudly on a classroom desk lid
Just
    As silence starts. *Who did that?* Well, he did.

We pull away to the hills, from where we see
    Thunder, dawn, or sheer
Emptiness unbolt the clouds, as the thing on high
    Has its one idea:
Catastrophe
    Somewhere or here.

The Devil bikes around, helping. He does!
    The Devil is not powerful. He cannot
Die. He steps on a mine, he stubs his toes.
    Like hell they hurt
But he bikes on. He goes
    To a gunman *Have a heart!*

He tries
    To free some hostages. He throws his arm
Round homesick Irish, Spanish, Canadian UN guys
    Who wake up in alarm
Alone, in the cold sunrise.
    He does no harm.

He is spotted moving across
    A no–man's–land while corporals scream *Go back!*
And bullets criss-cross
    His mending heart, which can only ache
Or endure loss,
    And is black.

We lose the Devil
    During a siege, but he crops up now in a newsreel
Trying with a Red Cross man to heave some rubble
    Off a shop girl,
But unable,
    And unhopeful.

The Devil we freeze in a frame
    Is stepping back, too tired,
Hands on his head. The Devil is doing the same
    Every day, while the Lord
Locks the gates of a camp, apportions blame,
    Gives His Word.

Car Game

His first he said was in HONOUR but not in GLORY.
He steered through the shattered village.
His second was not in SALT nor was it in PEPPER.
We were no wiser.
We passed a place-name slashed with a thick red line
To say that was it, gone, over.

His third, and we sucked our peppermints as he drove,
Was in both RHYME and RHYTHM.
We went by a farm and his fourth was not in FARM
But was in FERME.
'No?' he taunted, expecting us to be guessing
In his sickeningly warm

Old Citroën, and his fifth was not in SIGHT
But was in SPRIGHTLINESS
Of all things and we climbed a desolate hill.
I was unwell,
What with the churning and turning and him with his sixth
In JACK but not in JILL.

The tollbooth was abandoned, and we slid
The faces on our passes
Back inside our coats, then out again
To swap and grin.
His seventh was not in TIME or SPACE. Someone
Yawned 'What is it then?'

In vain of course. We could feel him smile. By now
We were out of the worst of it,
Unless it had spread this far. His last was in GOD
And CLOUD, he said.
His clue was 'We're for it now', so I said 'Homeland'
And watched his still grey head.

A Gate to the West

In are the sweet, the welcome flavours, in
Melt the appealing, the textured soften, all
Decreasing to luck, to a tiny sugary tide
Below one blissful tongue, that licks like a whole
Cat. The mouth is empty and satisfied.

A carious molar rocks at the brink of there.
Under and either side it is riddled with pain.
Love has done this, blurt the appalled insides,
Shutting their lips on air. When they part again
It will be to binge, alone, not telling where.

The People's Cinema

As blank as scripture to a ruling class
Discussed in hells they do not think exist,
Cracked and abandoned to the slicing grass
    And disabusing dust,
A movie screen shows nothing in a morning mist.

Here's where the happy endings were never had,
Or, like the long and lonely, never shown.
No one rode to the rescue of who was good,
    No star was born, none shone,
No dream came true, or fun began, or life went on.

A Classical outside. Like a parthenon
Or meant to be, but more as if that mother
Had quite disowned this worn and woebegone
    Shell of light. Its father
Was a woman's face in a glass. She ordered it like weather.

Here's where the stepping leg of a pale princess
Would never gleam in the flank of a silver Merc,
No carpet lap at the tips of an angel's dress
    As that began its catwalk,
No head be turned or heart won, none have all the luck.

It had to open faster than today.
She scratched a deadline on the skin of earth.
They couldn't meet it but they couldn't say.
    They swallowed back their breath.
The sun abruptly set in each unchewing mouth.

Here's where the plans were laid, and here ignored,
Here they were changed, here lied about, here lost,
Here's where they pulled the trick they could afford,
    Here's where they paid the cost,
Where a workman sang all day, baked in a wall to the waist,

When every short cut snapped on the one night,
Caving and bulging floors like a bigger child
Had waded from the future for a fight,
    And each thing was spilled,
Each dimly praying gap of air was found and filled.

The light went out on no one knows how few:
Interred, incinerated, a foot stuck out
Live from a ceiling waving in a shoe
    As the auditorium set,
And the sun was down, and the building up, and the deadline met,

And no one goes there now except to nod.
At what you get when men take on the sun.
At what men do when told to by a god
    Who's gone, and wasn't one.
How riches look in daylight when there *are* none.

The Clearest Eyes

The clearest eyes in our dear hemisphere
Could make out that the x of army plane
That is an answer to what is a prayer
Took off last night in silence from Orion.

Sulk

What we are at is pining for our lost
  Future. How we are doing that is simple:
Slouching beside our low glass tables dressed
    In shimmering precious suit from nape to ankle.

That's how it was to have been. The walls of silver,
  The doors that slish behind, the ultramarine
Drink, the apotheosis of the letter
    Z in Christian names and the light this clean.

Instead it's a sulk we'll have. We're the spoiled child
  With centuries for uncles, and those uncles
Leaning along the shelves disabused and old
    And letting us learn or not from the foul troubles

They dumped on us. Well we're not going to bother.
  We're going to sit here in our suits and shine,
Move and amend and move and adjourn forever,
    And pour the green olorosos of the moon,

Aren't we, Zardoq, though till the yawn of Time
  The rough and the brown and sick make war and changes
Backwards into the country, into the storm,
    And cluster there by the millpond of the ages.

The Sarajevo Zoo

Men had used up their hands, men had
offered, cupped, or kissed them to survive,
had wiped them on the skirts of their own town,
as different men had shinned up a ladder and taken
     the sun down.

One man had upped his arms in a victory U
to a thousand others, to show how much of the past
he did not know and would not know when he died.
Another's joke was the last a hostage heard:
     Oh I lied

which did win some applause from the bare hands
of dozing men. And others of course had never
fired before, then fired, for the work of hands
was wild and sudden in those days
     in those lands.

For men. For the women there was
the stroke, the ripping of hair, the smearing of tears,
snot, and there was the prod of a shaking man,
or with fused palms the gibbering prayer
     to the U.N.

The nothing they had between those palms was
hope and the yard between surrendering palms
was hope as well. Far off, a fist in the sky
was meaning hope but if you prised it open
     you saw why.

The hands of the children here were wringing themselves
hot with the plight of animals over there,
and drawing them in their pens with the crimson rain
of what men do to each other on television
     crayoned in.

But hands continued to feed the demented bear
who ate two other bears to become the last
bear in the Sarajevo Zoo. And they fed him
when they could, two Bosnian zookeepers
    all autumn.

Today I read that that time ended too,
when fifteen rifles occupying some thirty
hands got there and crept in a rank on knees
towards the smoke of the blown and stinking cages
    and black trees.

Trees were what you could not see the starving
beasts behind, or see there were now no beasts,
only the keepers crouching with their two lives.
Then winter howled a command and the sorry branches
    shed their leaves.

Yellow Plates

The family moving into the house were told
    To make themselves at home.

But dropping their things in a heap in the bare centre
    Of the largest, warmest room,

They had wondered how in hell they could cook a meal
    For twelve in a strange kitchen

(What with the brothers so drunk on the national drink
    And the grandchildren

Wailing the infant anthems *Why is nobody*
    Looking at me alone

Or *Take the others away until I need them*
    Or *What's undone's undone*)

But they found the cooking terribly easy, for here
    Was a fridge, a working oven

With even a clock, and here was a pile of matching
    Yellow plates: five, six, seven.

The Allies

Us? We were with the Allies. We were with you
Right on the dot, throughout, and we were with you
At and beyond the end. We were with the Allies.

And when we were with you we felt we were something more
Than a nation, we were a brotherhood, a cause.
Nobody said we flouted or broke things.

The enemy had one eye, though, that was simple.
It's hard to know what's right till the night you know
What wrong is and the enemy was what wrong is.

You great big nations thought of us and said 'Them?
They're with the Allies.' So we got added to prayers.
The name of our land was mouthed before the Amen

By your fair little children. In their schools
They crayoned us in like everyone, in the colour
The Allies were, and did projects on our products.

They told their mothers the things we make, but their mothers
Showed them them in tins. They had bought our products
Because we were allies. We were the Allies' allies.

After, we made our way to the capitals
Of superpowers, observed by the delicate ladies
Who live in them, and one told another one 'Them?

They were with us,' and that was like having new friends
Always passing, too well-bred to wave back.
Stroll by the Jubilee Arch as the sun goes down:

Ours are the curious names on the marble walls
As high as the eye can see. You have to remember
Our language has no vowels but it can be mastered.

Oh yes, we were with the Allies. Me myself?
I'll tell you about my war and about my wife
And daughters too if this fellow will ever serve me.

Queen of the Mice

Though there is nothing up, they do not know
    Exactly how it began, what gate or cavity
    Or agent error swallowed it into the town,

Though there is nothing up. They will poise them round
    To state as much at one and six and ten.
    Denials slide in print down a conveyor or

Swirl upscreen and show there is nothing up with a
    Blank scream and you know there are always some
    Scaremongers in fact there is always one of you

Look what happened. The mice or man they are bringing
    To solve what is not a problem does not arrive
    Until it is not and the Gallery has some two

Queries to which he can answer *No* and *You.*
    There is nothing up all day and darling believe
    There is nothing up all night. There is nothing up

With what comes back with an eye he covers and mutters
    Coast is clear, they are fine, they are fine as who
    Utter from manholes *help him* and disappear,

Untroubled as any who nose the remains of a meal
    Under a bridge, and blissful as life's canaries
    Ducking the air and making no other comment.

They are equally healthy who hang out,
    Hands in pockets, disabused, in the wind,
    Nor are they shocked who pause to putt in the distance,

Beam or denounce or hurry across this carpet.
    There is nothing up with the mice in their customary
    Crannies of the Mouse and Queen, smoking

Embassies, and Futures spring to mind
    As digits dance ahead and the Old Quarter
    Of Babylon goes *boom-boom* at the point of a gag.

There is nothing up with the dots that are not to blame.
    There is nothing up with the fauna liberally coated
    In After Eight and the fires you might see

Are not burning. Some of you may find
    Some of these pictures shocking but only some
    Pictures and only some of you because nothing

Is up I repeat and the Queen of the Mice and his friend
    The Queen of the Mice and his friend the Queen of the Mice
    Replace their phones on the earth and scramble high

Over the golden gases, the insect trials, high
    Over the pool where nothing was up, on a monster
    Gantry known as Agenda, soothe and resume,

And tiny up there, build their cereal cities,
    Crook their necks to that life-prolonging
    Fibre régime.

A Force That Ate Itself

They had marched on crust an infinitude of miles
    Eleven abreast. Just
Pages and pages of mud to read on the heels
    Of the one in front. They went
      As far as the eye could see, as far
        As the eye could bear.

Life in the force was hard and special, the time
    Empty of women. Someone
Tried aloud to remember them, but the same
    Silence fell like a quill
      Responding to a plea for love
        In the negative.

Gone were the crowd and gone were the enemy
    Months ago. There was no
Danger at hand or ahead, no charge or mêlée,
    No line to cross or cross
      To hold aloft, or peace to keep,
        Or war to stop;

Only the march of the only army there was,
    Eleven abreast. Just
Trudging the world in a line to endless applause
    From the last god, Mud,
      The Caliban in love below
        Who won't let go.

They trod the world so small the men they found
    Up ahead, quite mad,
Were their own tail but they cut them to the ground
    In innocence, and once
      Begun it could not be stopped, not until
        Each General

Had shot himself from behind and shuffled on.
　　This, luckily, would be
Impossible on our Earth, where no man
　　　Can catch himself himself,
　　　　But some can tear each other in half
　　　　　So don't laugh

At a world that had forgotten it was round.
　　Now it's a small brown ball,
And the muck of its surface thinks with a giggled sound
　　　Of the weight of men, of a time when
　　　　War went briskly through the crops
　　　　　With high hopes.

Ost

In Berlin,
    On a tiled, echoing street in the east, a spare
Long street,

A hairless man.
    Strapped in his leather, badges and insignia
Done to scare,

Jerks his walk
    Towards this lean approaching gastarbeiter
Brown with scorn,

And eyes catch,
    And for either to stop dead now is going to be too
Significant,

For the German,
    A drop of unusable oil from a functioning
Big gun,

Or the working
    Iranian, eyes down and eyebrows glistening
Rain or shine,

So on they come,
    Near, staring, semi-circling, back on,
On through Berlin,

And thus they say:
    Brother, when all my friends are here, you me
We do our act,

Enter to cheers,
    Lit by the spots of the world, expected to sing,
And obliging,

Our theme songs,
    Pricking to tears our people, or picked out nightly
By great critics,

Listened to,
     Followed across this space by believing eyes,
The stars of this,

Twinned in this
     Central hatred, crucial to this structure,
And exiting,

Or dying,
     After the duel of total light and evil,
Eloquently,

With a couplet
     Softly placing the lid on human things,
Then a bow...

For now:
     Two boys with dog-eared manuscripts, shitting it,
In the wings.

The Altered Slightly

Hilarious to the virus that has spent
its infinite resources
concocting itself anew,

these healers, helicoptered into a war zone,
with helmets and a peace plan,
pound the maps in a shell of an HQ.

Under the microscope the enemies goggle
in yellow and red grease,
their tricorn shapes a shock, and somebody says

*That's them but if you look
they've altered slightly.* Good news for the sniper,
who sights the Muslim wandering up the road,

then sights the Christian limping in the gutter,
and cannot choose between them or to let them
come and have each other. The dead,

uniquely in the dark about who did it,
lie still as stone, mistaken for the hiding,
while somewhere in some dedicated rich

lab the virgin germs,
nervous in molecular pitch dark,
parachute into a slide of blood

and set to work.

Phaeton and the Chariot of the Sun

Fragments of an Investigative Documentary

I *Cine*

Cine, sliver of history. A few minutes
finish you off in a blare of white, and the scutter
and scutter and sigh, then the lamp on and the smiling
that something, at least, is over.

Cine, chopper of Time, mercurial
slitter, century shadowing through our light:
London's sepia scuttle, a toadstool whitens
Nevada. Colour – Zapruder.

Cine. A reel was found in a vault in a place
I happened on in the course of a search. This reel
was not – but is now – the object of that search
so it's over. Which is how

poetry works, by the way. Like cine film
it yields to the bright. Like cine film it is either
print or nothing, like cine film that nothing
is sky. Like cine film

it's made of children who run towards you and cry.

II *Epaphus*

That's him there,
late in the fragment, laughing with three friends
as he points out to our point of view some sight
we never share.

He smokes a long
sobranie it looks like, brags away at a girl
who tires of him by the look and turns to us,
licks out her tongue

and wanders up,
fanning a smirk. Now even the camera fumbles
as she approaches, she's almost filling the frame –
one wet black lip

loves us. After this
Epaphus posing with one friend only. Pale,
demurring, shrugging. Phaeton. Yes, for sure!
Freeze it. Yes,

Epaphus, his friend,
now drunk, shakes him and leers. Was this that time
he told him his father wasn't his father really
and Phaeton, stunned,

backed into space?
No, this time he grins. Phaeton, lifts
a fluted glass off a tray, downs it and grins
and sets his eyes

coolly on us,
on the lens, on the future – that hungry severity
of anything gone forever is shrinking us all
to eager toddlers

blinking back
into the flicker. He finishes up another.
His mouth is forming words while we hear nothing
but flutter and tick

then our lens
fixes on him, doesn't mean to be caught up
but jams and is. A blot spreads out of the centre
and it all burns.

III *The Horses' Mouths: Pyrois*

Film me in silhouette. I insist. I'm not
Them prancing nags. Is that thing rolling? No?
Good. It better not be. What you got,
Rothmans? Gimme. What do you want to know?

The boy. The boy in the chariot? Oh no.
Some things I crack about, some things I don't.
You learn the worst is never long ago.
We horses live our lives in the word *won't*

But you don't understand, you undergods.
Gimme the Bushmills. Woh, that hits the spot.
The boy in the chariot. Hell. It makes no odds.
It happened. Why? This isn't lit. Why not?

What was the story... Somebody made him think
His father wasn't his father? Right, so he snaps
And goes and gets his way. Dies in the drink.
Talking of which... No, you pedalling chaps

Think you're as free as air though you're made of earth.
You got to obey your whim like a whipped horse
Flies. That boy. He thought about his birth.
He wanted it again. He ran his course.

IV *The Spokesman of the Sun*

Good morning, I'm researching into the death
    of this boy, do you know him?
You shake your head, but don't even take a look
    at the picture – how can you tell?
Excuse me, but we know you were on duty
    the morning he came here,
so surely you can remember him, and his name,
    and his claim that he was the son –
ah, now we're getting somewhere – he was the son
    of the Lord himself? – now sir,
that's very expensive equipment, that, you shouldn't
    do that, sir, we have to
suspect you if you won't assist us at all
    in our enquiries. Now, –
get off my foot, please, sir. Thank you. We're merely
    asking you to recall
the morning when this boy came here, we'd like
    the viewers to know exactly
how he came to be in control of equipment
    he couldn't possibly – sir,
that's not very nice, that, sir – he couldn't possibly –
    several thousand lives
depended on him, and all we want to know is
    how and why they had to
because of the negligence of your organisation
    die in horrific
sir, don't point that thing – okay, we're going!
    but thank you for your help,
I don't think – okay, we're going, we're going!
    – Fuck me, did you see that?
He would have used it, too. We're out of here.
    I don't know. Some day
this work is going to get me killed, I swear.

How did you find me here?
     This is my refuge from all human voices,
     Their differences that shrivel into hisses
All indistinct, their faces
     Merged to the infinite grains of a far shore

Licked by the dog sea.
     Here on my noiseless meadow I ride alone,
     Ride, ride myself with the wind on my spine,
While the fuelled and roaring Sun
     Mislays my name in the mess of his tyranny.

Talk to the others, friend.
     Find the unkempt Pyrois; Aethon, vain
     And cosseted by Man, then look for Phlegon
Anywhere where the thin
     Are all there is, and the wind is a hurled sand.

That's his gesture. Mine?
     Mine's this solitude. I've a world to tell
     But not this world. We switched your sky into Hell
And all for a human will,
     Its pride, its point, its prick. It will come again.

How did I know it was him?
     When we were torn through clouds and the East Wind
     I felt no weight on my back, heard no command,
And felt no pull, no hand,
     No pilot. No escape now. Kingdom come.

Three images, that's all.
     One was his face, the boy, his face when he lost
     The reins and then his footing – that was the last
We saw of him – he must
     Presumably have gone in a fireball –

Another was how the Moon,
      Seeing us hurtle by, reminded us all
      Of the face of a mother beside a carousel,
Worrying herself ill,
      As her children wave, are gone, are back too soon –

And another was afterwards.
      I lay for a good forever somewhere in a woods.
      The petrified seconds prayed, the hours wore hoods.
'You gods,' I said, 'you gods.'
      And those, I trusted, those were my final words

To men. Instead, these are:
      Forget Eous, leave me alone in my meadow,
      Riding myself, racing my sisterly shadow
Into the shade, where sorrow
      Wraps her and deserts me, drenched, here.

VI *Mulciber*

The Palace of the Sun. Item. Gates of.
All things are made of what I say they're made of.
The heavens, earth and fire are made of silver.
The sea is made of gods. The gods, however,
Themselves are made of silver. This is Triton.
What do you mean 'It's Saturn'? Nothing like him.
This is Aegeon, riding on two creatures.
Whales, you reckon? Well, they got whale features
But they ain't whales. Whales is made of blubber.
Prick this skin of a bark you've silver rubber.
Besides, you enter the legend as a vandal.
That's Proteus on the left, on the right, in the middle –
Ho! He's where I say he is. His positions
Alter daily. Simplest of commissions.
Doris rides on fishback, while her daughters
Dry their hair forever, like my daughters.
Meanwhile, back on the land, the men are manly,
The beasts are beastly, the cities urban. Only,
The sky's a bit of a solo spot for the craftsman:
Virgin, Scales, Scorpion – see yours? – Bowman,
Goat and Waterman, then on this right-hand panel
More bloody Fish, Ram, Bull, Twins (mine was the model:
One son, two images! Clever, eh?) then the Pincers,
Then old Laird of the Woods. Oh and manifold dancers,
All-purpose Nymphs and Shepherds. Sightsee's over.
That concludes your visit to *World of Silver*.
Fill in the yellow form in the Antechamber
If you're interested in becoming a Silver Member.
No cameras, thank you, sir. No we don't discuss
That. We don't take questions from the Press.
There was in fact no boy and no such flight.
Research was done. Not one thing came to light.
I showed you the Silver Gate. That's what I'm for.
And now I'm showing you the silver door.

One minute, love.
You're looking at
The winner of
The 2.15,
3.38
And 5 o'clock.
I haven't time.
I race, I work.

Ask what you want
But ask it fast.
The time you spend
Is time I lose,
Is time we've lost.
Aethon never
Loses, friend,
You got that? Ever.

The chariot?
The idiot boy?
I don't admit
And never shall
I lost that day.
He may have done.
He burned. So what?
His father's son.

The countries burned,
The oceans steamed,
The stinking wind
It filled my eyes.
I never dreamed
Years afterwards
I'd humble all
These thoroughbreds

Day in day out,
Year after year,
Beyond all doubt
Beyond compare,
The sight they fear,
Aethon, pride
Of any course
You humans ride.

If all the gold
That lights this room
Was melted, rolled
And stretched for me,
I should in time
Reach Heaven's Gate
And there I'd not
Be made to wait

But rode by servants
Back to where
I rode the Heavens
Once, the Sun
Would part the air
For Aethon,
Fanfared, forgiven
Aethon.

VIII *A Scientist Explains*

Would he have suffered? That depends what you mean.
Would he have suffered? Lady, let me explain.

    The fire went north.
    The northern Plough,
    Too hot to bear it,
    Plunged below
    The sea; the Snake,
    Sluggish and cold,
    Was scorched to fury,
    Boötes, old
    And slow, he too
    Was stricken down,
    He too was dragged or stricken down
    When Phaeton flew.

Would he have suffered? Suffering's hard to define.
Would he have suffered? Lady, let me explain.

    He was afraid
    Of heights and now
    The world he knew
    Was spread below
    And churning. West
    He'd never make,
    The wounded East
    Bled in his wake.
    He didn't know
    The horses' names,
    He'd never thought to ask their names
    And didn't now.

Would he have suffered? Would he have suffered pain?
Would he have suffered? Lady, let me explain.

    He bore the worst
    Of Heaven, curved
    With poison – Scorpio!
    Wild, he swerved

And lost the reins
And lost the flight,
The chariot set
This world alight:
The woods and streams,
The crops and towns,
The nations perished in their towns
As in their dreams.

Would he have suffered? That depends what you mean.
Would he have suffered? Lady, let me explain.

Athos, Taurus,
Helicon,
Parnassus, Cynthus,
Babylon,
Ossa, Pindus,
Caucasus,
Olympus, Libya,
Ismarus,
Rhine and Rhône
And Nile and Tiber,
Nile and even promised Tiber?
Steam on stone.

Would he have suffered? Suffering's hard to define.
Would he have suffered? Lady, let me explain.

The seas had shrunk
And all was sand,
They felt the scorch
In Netherland;
Nereus sweltered,
Neptune swore,
The Earth appealed
High Jupiter:
'I may deserve
This doom, but spare
Your Heaven itself from fire, spare
What's left to save!'

Would he have suffered? Would he have suffered pain?
Would he have suffered? Lady, let me explain.

Obviously
One shot alone,
One thunderball
From Heaven's throne
Divided boy
From flaming car,
Made fire of him
And falling star,
A star of him
That plunged and died
In the River Eridamus, died
Far far from home.

Would he have suffered? That depends what you mean.
Would he have suffered? Lady, let me explain.

Lady?

IX *Clymene's Coda*

Death was instantaneous.
Death is always instantaneous.
Loss was instantaneous.
Loss is always.

Get on my back. You all do in the end.
You've come some way to go the way you came,
    But shall do, all the same,
    My doubly hopping friend,
At least you ride in peace, at least you ask my name.

Where are the other three? There's no surprise.
Eous rippling aimlessly alone,
    Pyrois wrecked, Aethon?
    Neighing at blue skies,
As if his loss, our loss, was some grand race he'd won.

I work this zone. Don't have to, but I do.
I do have to, and so would you. Look now,
    The planters on the brow,
    They falter, wondering who
Wants what of them and why. They'll try to question you.

Be plain with them. It waters you with hope
That in this desert where the fire can't die
    Nor air reach to the sky,
    Somehow they grow a crop
That doesn't care it's dead, that doesn't know. Now stop,

Get off my back. Feel hotness on each sole
And howl. For this is not the word made flesh,
    This is the word made ash,
    This is the mouth made hole,
Here where the star fell, here where he got his wish.

XI *Burned*

These are what we plant.
    This is what we grow.
These are what we eat.
    This is what we know.

Nobody will come
    With any more to plant.
Those who come will come
    With bags, because they want

What we have left to eat.
    This is what we turn.
This is what we pay
    Out of what we earn.

These are what we plant.
    This is what we grow.
These are what we eat.
    This is what we know.

Whatever cross we pray to,
    Whatever cross we bear,
You are earthmen, you are earthmen
    And you do not care.

XII *Phaeton and the Chariot of the Sun*

Into the eye of my world
    Falls, glinting, the light of my father.
Never again shall I doubt
    That the crown I can feel is intended
But for Phaeton his son,
    I, pride of the fabulous morning.
Warm in my room I await
    The procession of brightening beauties:
She at their head who will hope;
    She, fair, who will pray to no purpose;
She near the end who'll be flung
    On the cold yellow coast of the jealous;
Soft and unique at the end
    Sighs she who is fit for Phaeton.

Cold in the day I will stare
    At the clouds that have gathered for nothing,
Nothing but murmur and doubt
    At the power and pain of my coming,
Melting the solemn away,
    I, son of all light and all loving!
Where are the arrogant now?
    Where, when, will they suffer Phaeton?

Hurt in the night I can hear
    Hooves, falls in the chase of my heartbeat.
I am the one who will loom
    As a tower at the end, though my wishes
Whiten the world like a star:
    Clouds, enemies, rivals, tremble!

Out of the night I will ride,
    Burning bright through the eye of my father.
Watch me until I am gone,
    Friend. Watch me forever, and after.

Younger Than That Now

(for the Folk at the Barn)

Open the door one crack and you are backstage.
The closest of the bright unanswering faces
You love and know, but away down the crowded passage
They get much gloomier, longer to recognise.
      Your shyly whispered guesses

Widen and die like cigarette fumes in a hall
Of cleanly livers. You did not know you were holding
Your breath when it broke clear, and there is no wall
To touch, there are only inhabited crackling clothes
      And soon the dizzying feeling

That you must walk through here through the way of them all:
The girls of the frozen chorus, the mouthing page,
The hero bare, the jacketed devil, the cool
Chanel of the goddess, the flirt of the woods, pass on
      Away from the terrible stage

That grinds its young in the light or blows them dark
Like birthday candles, move down corridors
Where the murdered glance from a brilliant mirror and back,
By vast and icy rooms with bills of plays
      That call you to old wars,

Past centuries of dresses coldly hung
In line, rich girls speechless at the affront,
And cards of luck and photographs of song
Pinned to a blistered board, pass by the wires
      That lead from what you want

Away to the grids and terminals of power,
Pass by yourself in brown and broken glass,
By planks and crates at the foot of a storage tower,
By what seems rubbish to you but will be of use,
      And then the rubbish. Pass

Right to the end of the theatre, some last
Green paint-spattered chair by a bolted door.
Far from the lives of the young indignant cast
Or wrenching earshot of beloved lines,
    Sit yourself down there.

Feel like a boy the burden tremble and slip.
Empty your pockets of work and empty your ears
And nose and eyes of fashion. Summon up
Whatever remains. If nothing remains amen,
    But blink no appealing tears,

For here you sit in the foreground of the world.
And what you sing in the dark is the plain song
Of men alone: unobservant, innocent, old,
And blue with wonder, and beating a way back home,
    And over before long.

The Sightseers

We sing, we lucky pirates, as we sail,
Overladen with our creaking cargo
Of eights and nines, and imagine chains of island
Zeroes up ahead. Some of us are ill, though,
And yelp and gibber of a rushing edge,
A foam of stars, the boatswain upside down
Who grins *You told me so.*
                                        We draw to the rail,
Sleepless, and we wait, and, sure enough,

Behind us like our chat against the breezes,
They stir and mutter, whom we call the Sightseers,
Who stay the length of a hundred of my heartbeats.
No time at all with the Sightseers behind us.

I count the beats, it's how I'm brave enough
Not to cry out or vault the rail for terror –
I number them as years of the dim hundred
Soon to be gone: so I have them born to sunlight,
Then growing in that apple England, picked
Or fallen, then I think of them as upright,
Ideas and expectations trailing off
Across the years, and then I see them cold,
Unshockable and tired. And by the time I

Stumble in on the sixty-second heartbeat
Their eyes are red with secrets, and their heads
Are white with what is put from an honest mind.
And then they don't believe what they are seeing.
And then they are seeing nothing, and I believe

They walk on deck because they wake and sniff
Some empty space at every century's end,
Like breath gone out, or the air of the first flowers
That ever filled their eyes, as if it's starting –
They jolt from bed and hurry from their cabins

To see strange figures clutching at a rail.
We sing, we lucky pirates, as we sail.

112